Circle Boy and Triangle Girl

Jordin Good

Published in 2023
First published in the UK by THP Kidz Zone
An imprint of Tamarind Hill Press Limited
Newton Aycliffe, County Durham, DL5 6XP
Copyrights © THP Kidz Zone
All rights reserved

Created by Jordin Good
As part of the *"Well Rounded Child"* series.

ISBN: 978-1-915161-84-0

Printed and manufactured by Lightning Source LLC

Circle Boy and Triangle Girl
Talking About Moods and How You Feel!

This book belongs to:

_____

Circle Boy and Triangle Girl played together in a swirl.
Happy and bouncing, full of glee,
they danced around a big oak tree.

But one day, Circle Boy's mood was not as bright and true.

Triangle Girl noticed his frown, and asked him what brought him down.

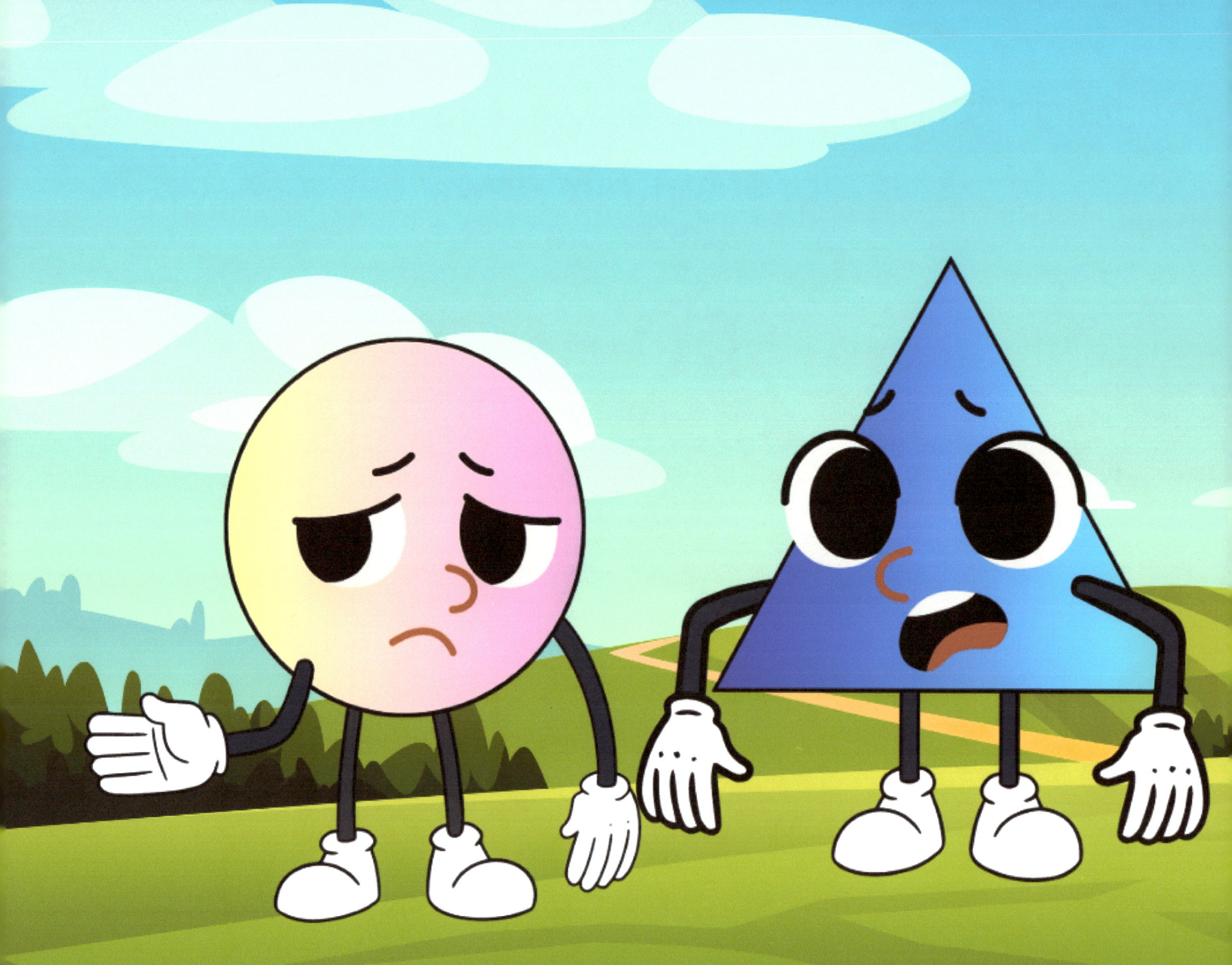

Circle Boy said, "I don't know why, but sometimes I feel like I could cry. I wish I could be happy like you, but today I am feeling kind of blue."

Triangle Girl replied, "It's okay to feel sad or angry sometimes. Everyone has different moods. On days when I'm feeling down, I like to turn it all around. I take a deep breath and count to three, and think of things that make me happy."

Circle Boy asked, "Can you show me how?"

"Sure, let's do it now! Take a deep breath, count to three, and think of things that make you happy," Triangle Girl answered.

Circle Boy closed his eyes and tried to think of things that made him feel alive. He thought of playing with his favourite toy and swimming in the pool with joy.

He opened his eyes with a smile and said, "Thank you! That took a while, but I feel much better now. I am glad I have a friend like you."

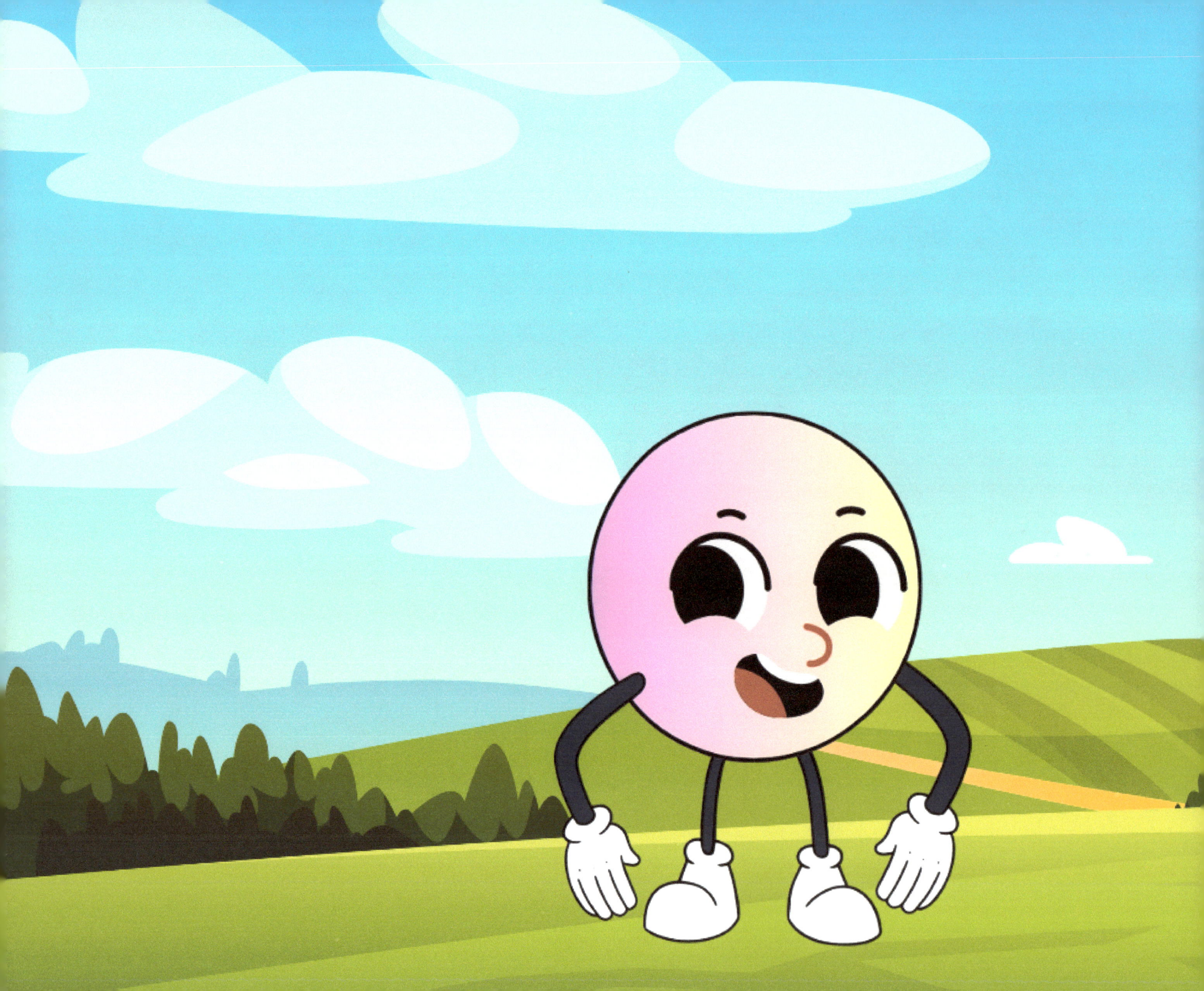

"You're welcome, friend. Remember, moods come and go. It's okay to feel happy or sad. I'll be here to support you either way," Triangle Girl reassured him.

As they played and laughed once more, Circle Boy felt better than before. He knew that his friend was right; moods can change from day to night.

Sometimes you'll feel happy and bright. Other days, you might feel a bit tight, but it's important to know, and see that your feelings are okay, no matter what you feel.

Circle Boy and Triangle Girl learned a lesson, that's for sure. Talking about moods and how you feel can make you happier than ever still.

The End.
#CBTGstory

www.ingramcontent.com/pod-product-compliance
Lightning Source LLC
Chambersburg PA
CBHW042108090526

44591CB00004B/45